Happy
FOR YOU

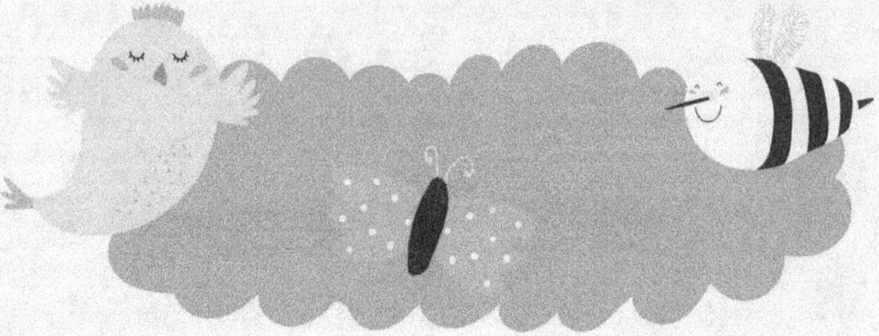

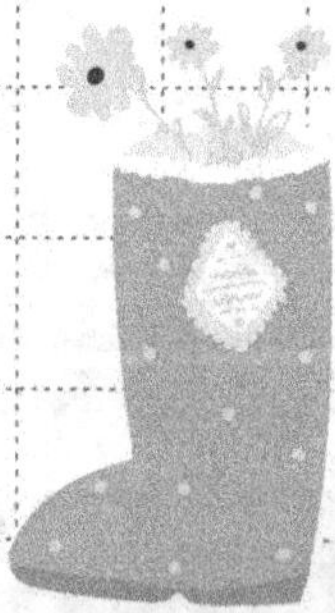

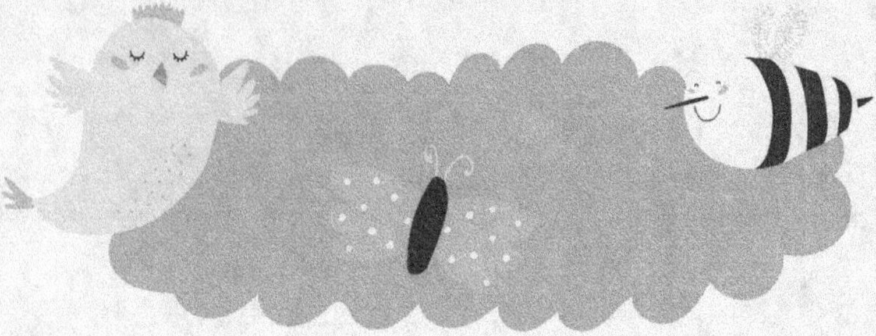

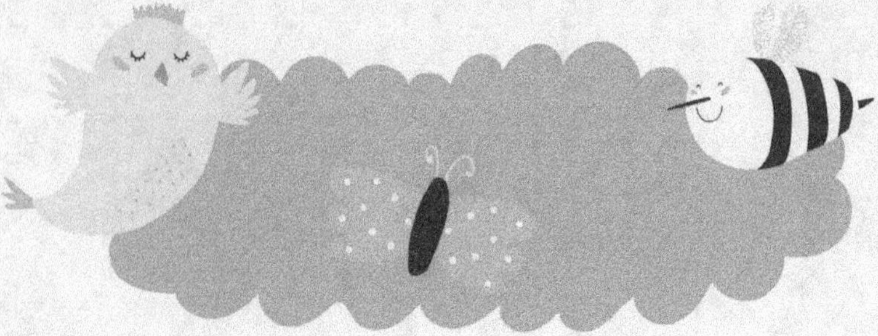

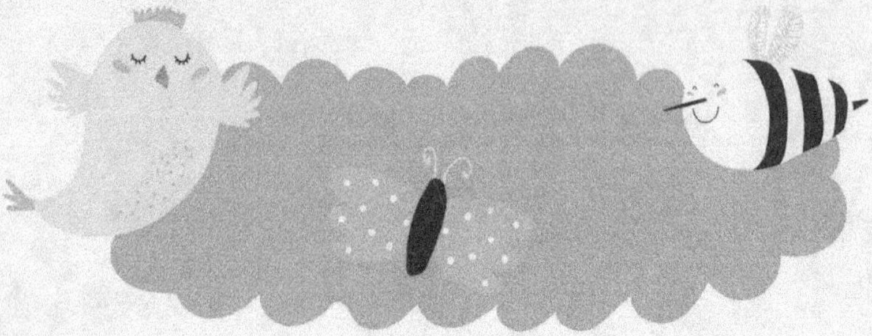

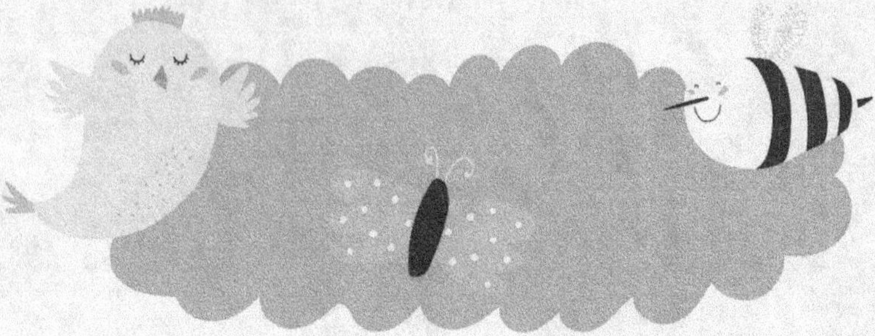

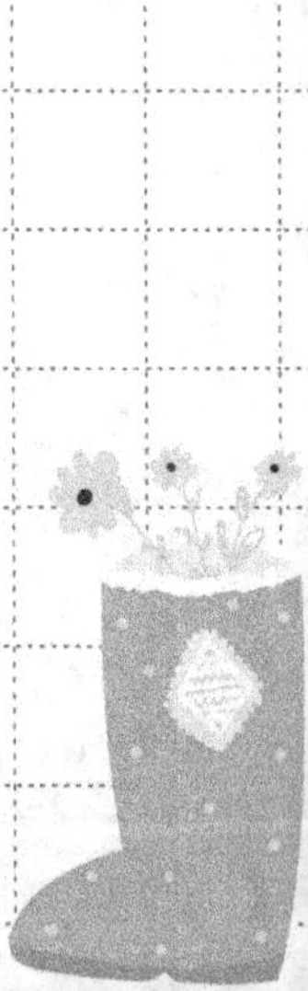

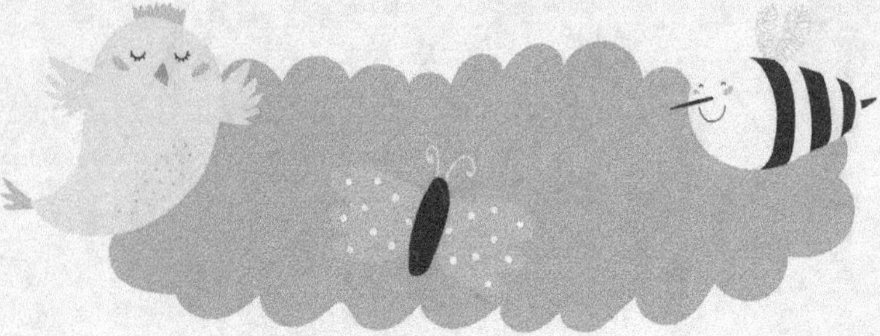

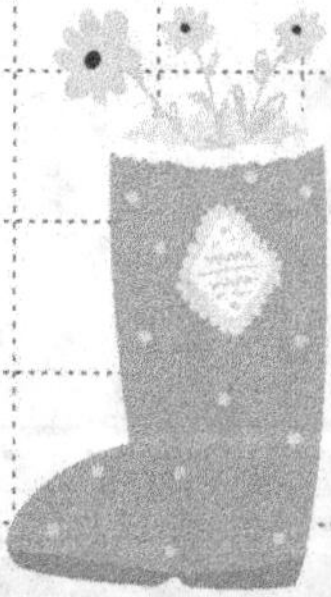

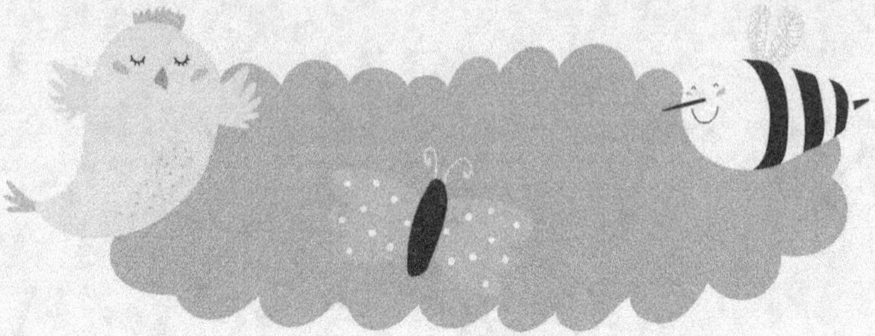

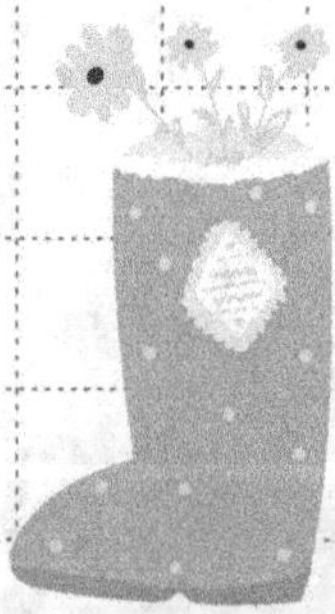

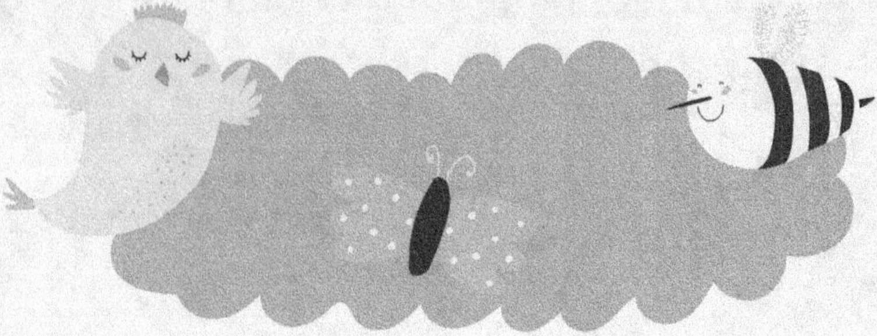

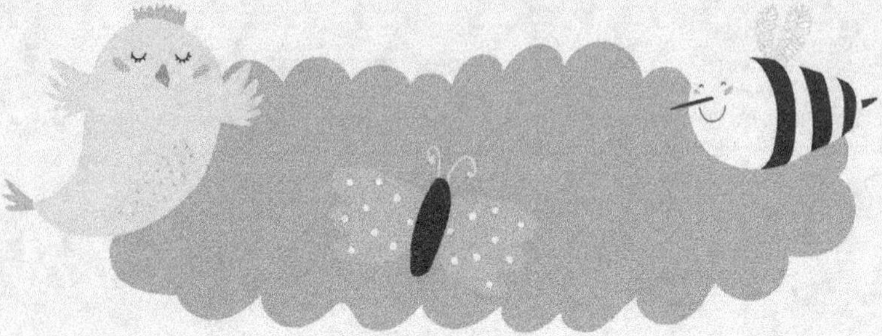

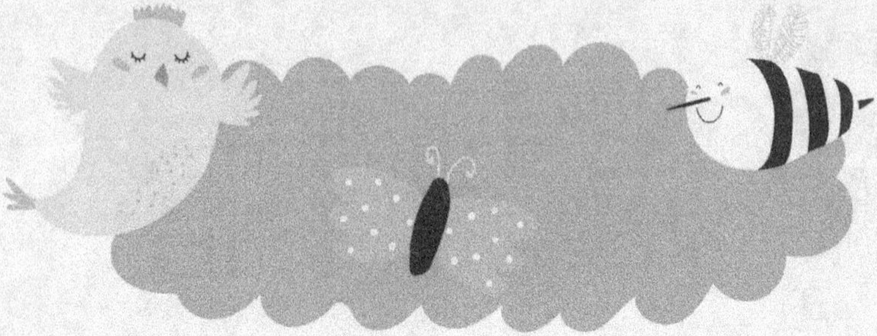

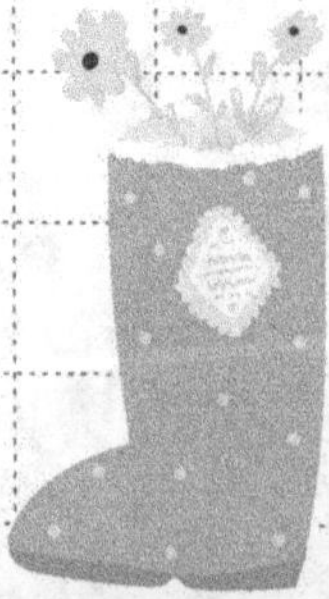

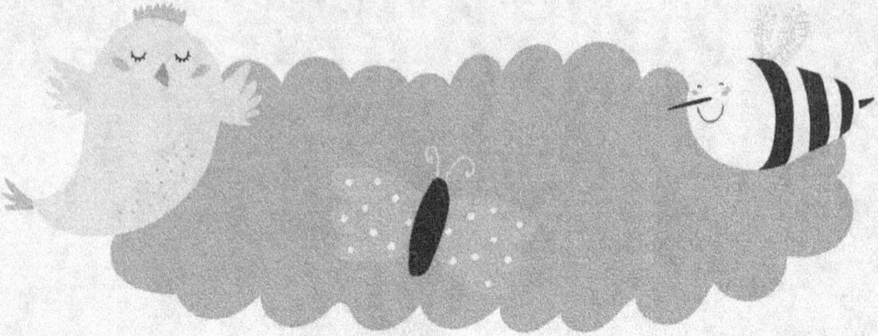

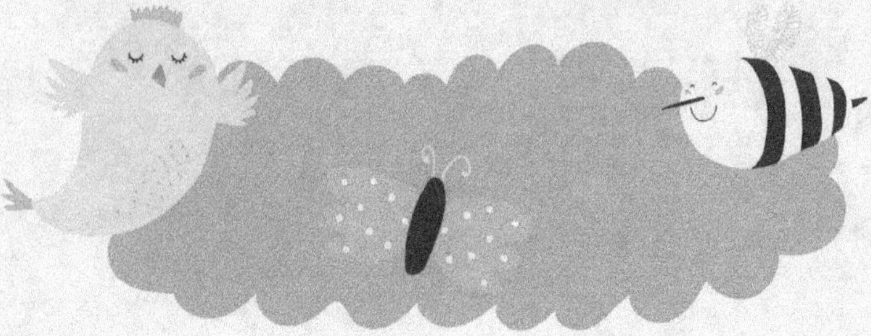

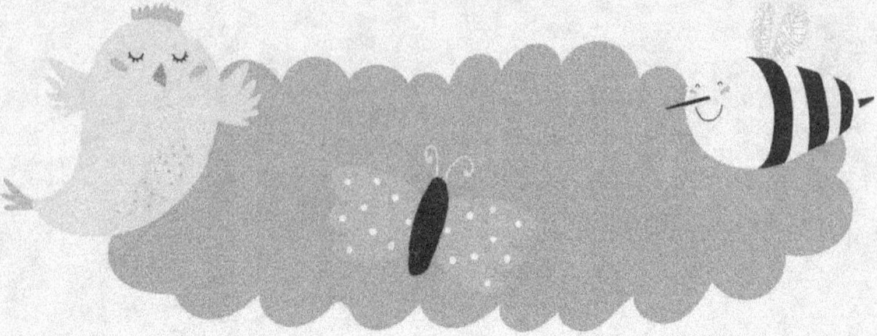

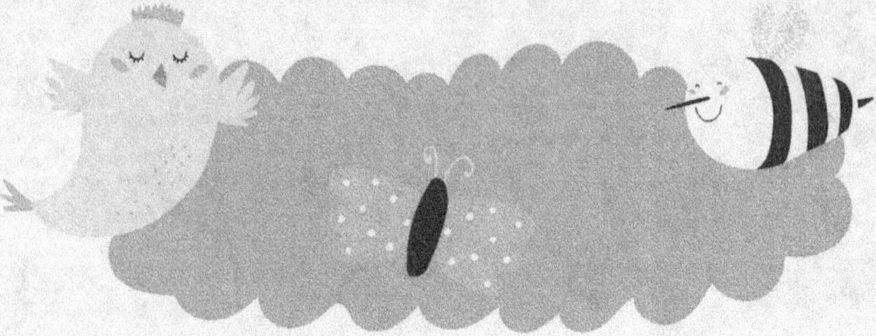

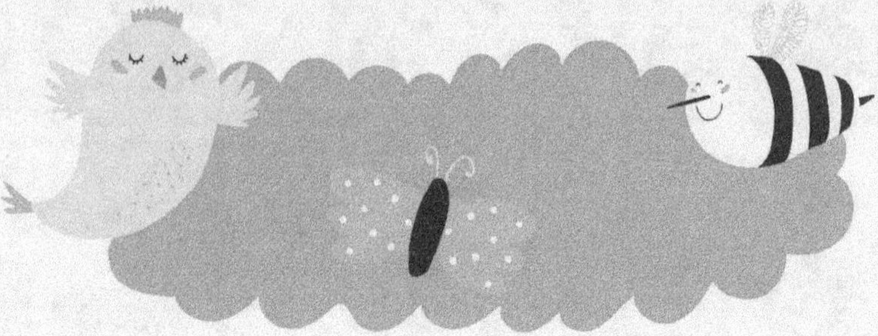

a little
Happy
FOR YOU

www.ingramcontent.com/pod-product-compliance
Lightning Source LLC
Chambersburg PA
CBHW070149080526
44586CB00015B/1914